4/87

Date Due

INFORMATION TECHNOLOGY

Design   Cooper–West   Consultant Jack Schofield
Editor   Margaret Fagan   Editor of the Computer Guardian,
Researcher Cecilia Weston-Baker   *The Guardian*, UK
Illustrator Rob Shone

Designed and produced by
Aladdin Books Ltd
70 Old Compton Street
London W1

*First Published in
the United States in 1986 by*
Franklin Watts
387 Park Avenue South
New York NY 10016

ISBN 0 531 10198 3

Library of Congress Catalog
Card Number: 86 50031

Printed in Belgium

MODERN
TECHNOLOGY
INFORMATION
TECHNOLOGY

DON SLATER

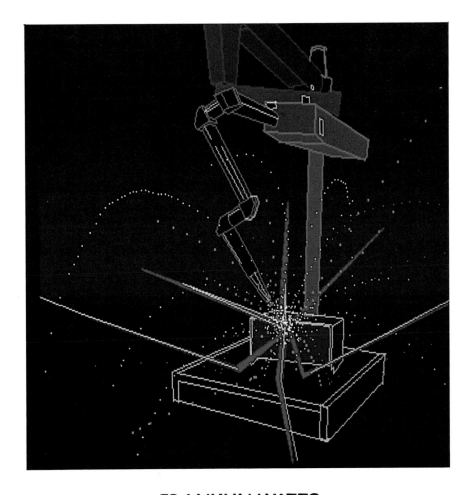

FRANKLIN WATTS
NEW YORK·LONDON·TORONTO·SYDNEY

Telephones linked to computers are the key to information technology

Introduction

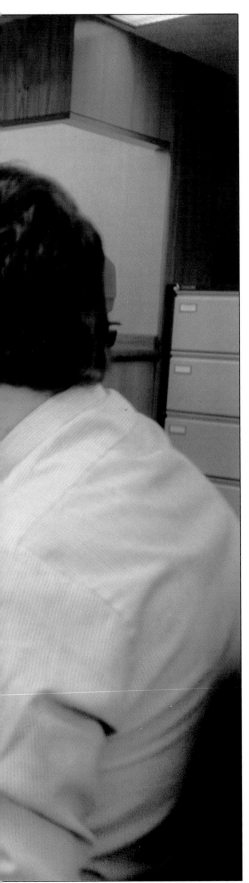

Information technology (IT) is about the different ways that information – words, images, sounds, numbers – can be handled electronically. In the past few years computers have become cheaper and more powerful. Today, telecommunications are becoming part of the computer world. Telecommunications are able to link up computers and to transmit information around the world at vast speeds.

IT is concerned with putting computers and telecommunications together into systems for handling information. This book examines the various IT systems and looks at how they are changing our ways of living and working.

Contents

The IT world

The IT world is growing rapidly. It now includes offices and factories, schools and hospitals, and even the home. The main reason for this growth is that IT can handle huge amounts of information quickly and flexibly. This information is stored on disks ready for recall at the press of a button. Combining information, such as images and texts, is made more efficient by IT. Most importantly, IT allows information to be communicated around the world.

Collecting information
Because information is so easily transmitted through the system, it can be collected at many different points. Home computers (3) can be used to link up to huge banks of information via the telephone line (6).

Storing information
Information storage (1) is central to IT. "Floppy disks" are the most common storage device for personal computers. Hard disks and magnetic tapes are more suitable for large systems. Information may be stored on your desk or in a database (2) across the globe.

IT communication links

6

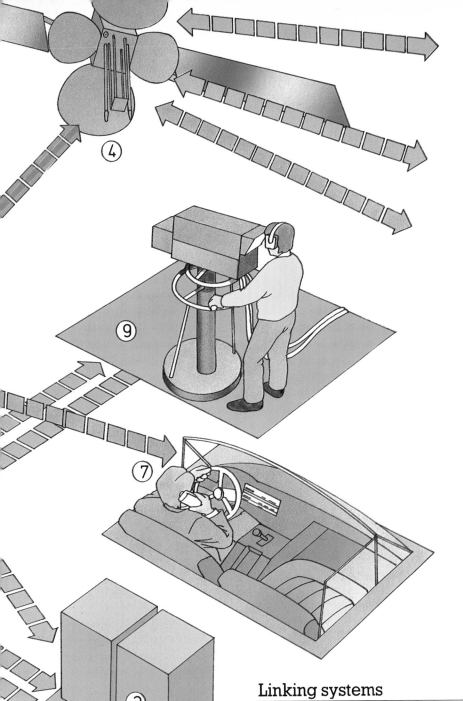

Moving information

Information is sent as electric pulses through cables. Satellites (4) allow data to be sent around the world almost instantly. Their signals are picked up by a communications dish (5) before being sent to wherever they are needed.

Telephones

Data can be sent to a computer through the telephone system (6). New portable telephones (7) allow communications from outside the office.

Television

In the IT world, televisions (8) do more than receive the broadcast channels (9), they can also send information. IT takes its place alongside hi-fi (10) and video (11) as home entertainment.

Newspapers and books

With IT, publishing is carried out electronically. Words and images are prepared and collected on computers, and only appear on paper at the very last stage (12). Readers can read books and magazines on computer screens or print them out at home.

Linking systems

Information technology is the product of "convergence." This means that previously separate technologies can be linked together to form a single system. The diagram shows how information can be sent down telephone lines to be collected in one place, worked on at another, and stored in a third. It also shows how television, videos and computers can be linked together so that images stored on one kind of machine can be mixed with words prepared on another. Through satellites and new forms of cable, computers can be linked into world-wide systems forming international offices and so any computer can communicate with any other.

What is information?

To keep modern societies running, many people need up-to-date facts, such as news, telephone numbers and prices. Businesses need information about sales, wages and costs. Governments need to know about such things as taxes and spending. IT systems store, process and transmit not only this type of knowledge but anything a computer can treat as information, such as photographs, music and voices. When this information is translated into electronic signals it can be processed very quickly.

▷ Computers can send and receive information down telephone lines. But to do this the digital code used by computers must be converted into the continuous signals telephones use to transmit voices. At the other end, the signals must be translated into digital code again for the receiving computer.

Digital information

IT systems work by reducing *all* information into the same type of computer code. An ordinary telephone translates the sound of your voice into electrical signals which vary as your voice does. But telephones can also be part of a "digital" system which measures these signals thousands of times every second and converts each signal into an "on/off" sequence of electrical pulses. It is this on/off sequence, called "binary code," which is understood by the computer.

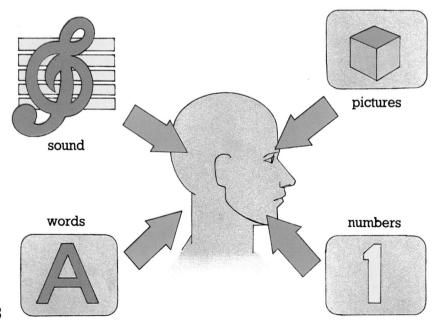

sound

pictures

words

numbers

◁ We are used to thinking of the sounds we hear, the images we see and the words we speak as different forms of information. To a computer, however, every type of information is the same – bundles of binary code which it can process, store or transmit. Because information is coded in the same form, it can be used anywhere within the IT system.

▷ Binary code has only two symbols, "0" and "1," which represent "off" and "on" — the presence or absence of a pulse of light or electricity. These pulses control the computer.

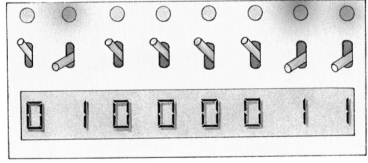

▽ A binary digit (a "1" or "0") is known as a "bit." Data can be sent down an ordinary telephone line at about 1,200 bits per second; a new digital line will carry 64,000 bits per second. It will also carry many more messages of this size at the same time. The diagram below shows how technology has speeded up the sending of information.

Time taken to travel 645 km (400 miles)

 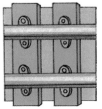 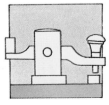 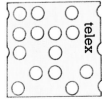 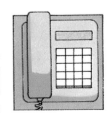 

10 days   10 hours   4 minutes   2 minutes   30 seconds   0.1-1 second   9

Communicating information

Telecommunications are becoming faster and more efficient. This is because telephone systems are changing to a digital basis. The telephone system will also be improved by the use of "fiber optics." Made from extremely pure glass, optical fiber has the advantage of being able to carry 500 times as many messages as an ordinary telephone line. An optical fiber signal traveling at the speed of light is the fastest and most efficient way of sending information.

Optical fibers have another advantage: they eliminate the few seconds delay experienced in satellite communication. Because they directly join two places on earth, the distance the signal has to travel is dramatically reduced.

▽ Optical fiber (seen in the photograph below) is made of tiny strands of glass. Signals are sent along the fiber as pulses of light which carry messages in digital binary code. The light pulses bounce along the fiber as shown in the diagram. Each fiber can carry 1,000 telephone conversations. A fiber optic cable consists of bundles of tiny strands. Optical fibers are more reliable than the bulkier electric cables used by conventional telephones.

optical fiber

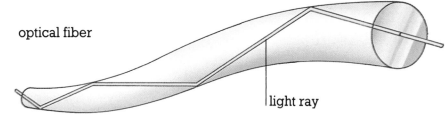

light ray

Satellite communication

△ Once the symbol of the future, satellites today are the basis of global communications. Each satellite has several channels which can handle thousands of messages at the same time. The diagram shows how satellites can be linked into networks which cover the entire earth. However, it is thought that fiber optics will eventually replace satellite communications.

The telephone revolution

Telephones and computers can be linked by a device called a "modem." This translates the computer's digital code into signals suitable for today's telephone. (A modem can be seen in the photograph on page 9 fitted beneath the computer.) Through telecommunications, a telephone linked to a computer by a modem can call up central information banks called "databases." The database could be in the same building or halfway around the world.

11

The electronic office

IT replaces paper work with electronic work. Information such as sales, salaries and the designs of products is keyed into a desktop computer called a "workstation." A workstation can combine a computer with a telephone, modem and other office equipment such as "teletex" and "fax." Teletex, a new high-speed message system, receives incoming messages while preparing outgoing ones. Fax allows pictures to be sent down telephone lines.

Office networks

In the modern office, local area networks, "LANs," link all electronic equipment into a single office system. A few giant companies own channels on satellites through which they can link up their offices around the world, thus creating a world-wide network. "Teleconferencing" allows executives to "meet" electronically by television link-up.

▽ The electronic office works as one large system. As well as normal telephone facilities (1), cables connect workstations to a large computer (2), which stores all the company's data. The various offices may hold teleconferences (3), or send documents or images by fax (4). Any terminal can receive information from distant computers (5). Portable computers (6) are used to send electronic mail – messages sent over the telephone lines. The office can be connected, through the telephone system or a satellite link (7), to other offices (8).

▷ People in different offices can hold meetings by teleconferencing – both sight and sound are transmitted by cable or satellite link. Though some companies have their own, lower-quality facilities, most use special studios.

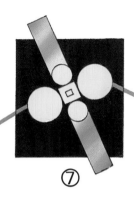

⑦

⑧

▽ Fax is used to transmit images, such as photographs, or exact copies of letters. The image is electronically scanned. Through telecommunications, it is sent to a terminal where it is printed out on paper. In this way "copies" can be sent instantly to anywhere in the world.

①

⑥

PitneyBowes

13

IT at home

IT has not yet made a great impact on homes. However, this is beginning to change. Inexpensive word processors, which can store texts so that they can be easily altered before being printed out, are beginning to replace typewriters. Simple IT like telephones with memories are becoming common. As modems become cheaper, people are beginning to explore the possibility of working at home on computers which are linked to an office by telephone. IT is also being used to link patients at home to hospitals. Cable television, which can allow viewers to send information, is becoming important. "Qube," an experimental scheme in the US, carries television, banking facilities and a home shopping service.

▽ Some people expect cable TV to be the basis for IT in the home. Copper cable or optical fiber can carry numerous signals, including television channels, directly into the home. Cable can also be "interactive" – information can be sent back along the cable. For example, some US cable companies allow viewers to vote on which of two or three possible endings they would like a TV program to have. However, as an IT system for the home, viewdata seems more promising.

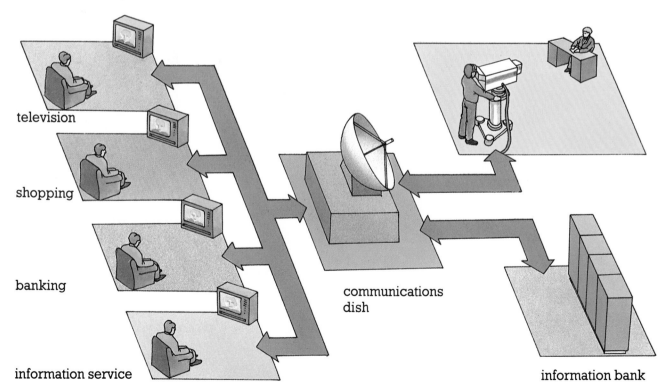

television

shopping

banking

communications dish

information service

information bank

▷ With "teleshopping," the users call up information about a product, make a choice and order the goods over viewdata. They can pay by credit card and the goods are either mailed or delivered to the home.

△ Viewdata systems like Prestel can hold millions of "pages" of data on their central computers. Users follow directories to find the page of information they want.

Shopping at home

The most useful example of IT in the home could turn out to be "viewdata." In viewdata systems like "Prestel" in the UK or "Captain" in Japan, television sets with keypads (remote control panels) are connected through the telephone system to a large information network. Viewdata is a two-way communication system: by using the keypad, it is possible to shop for goods or to manage your bank account from your own home.

IT in the street

Shopping involves a lot of information: prices, numbers of goods and sales. IT can help manage this electronically. For example, a system using "bar codes" printed on packages can tell a machine the price and type of product sold. By passing a "light pen" over the bar code, the cash register can add up the bill, and send sales and stock information to central computers. Similar systems can be used by libraries to check out books. IT can also distribute information – sales catalogues can be distributed on video disks and "touch screens" hooked up to video disks allow consumers to call up product demonstrations.

Check cards and credit cards

Ordinary check cards have magnetic strips which carry information such as a "PIN" – personal identification number. These cards can be used to withdraw money or check bank balances at cash dispensers. Machines are becoming available that can automatically check credit cards with a central computer.

▽ Cash dispensers are already widespread. New bank cards have both a magnetic strip and a hologram which contains the user's name, account number and PIN. A "smart card" can contain even more information: it can include whole programs, processors and memories and can be plugged into different computers. Cumana in the UK has produced a card which carries a complete program for word processing.

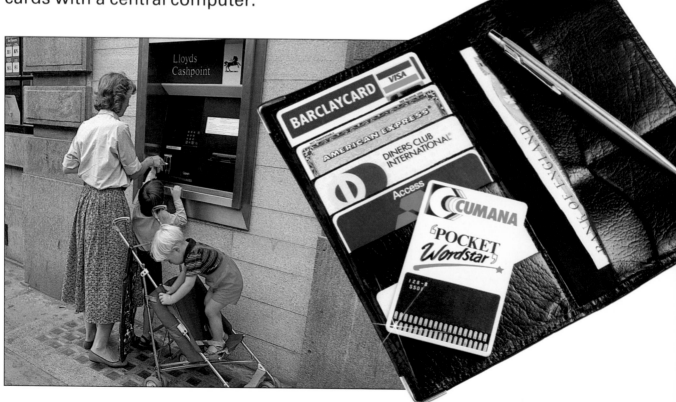

▷ Bar codes are simply machine-readable stripes of varying widths which can be printed on a product in normal ink. Supermarkets which use bar codes can present their customers with a bill which lists every item bought and its price. In the photograph above, the code is being read by a laser light.

bar code and light pen

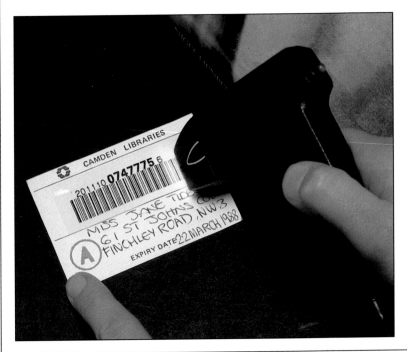

◁ A bar code scanner (light pen) is used to check a person's library ticket. The bar code allows for fast entry of data into the library's computer. A similar bar code appears on all books. The two bar codes are both stored by the computer to provide a record of books on loan and their date of return.

Interactive video

Video disks can hold vast amounts of digital information, either in text or image form, which can be viewed as still frames or moving pictures. The technology of "interactive video" allows users to plan their own route through the material stored on the disk: any image can be called up in any order using a keypad or computer.

Video disks are very useful for teaching because they allow students to "interact" with the computer. For example, a visual demonstration of how to set up a computer can be followed by questions answered through a computer keyboard. Depending on the answers given, the computer continues with a further explanation or a demonstration of the next step.

▷ A video disk or CD in a car can hold many thousands of maps which can be called up in a useful way for drivers. First look at a map of a large region, then call up the town you are approaching, and even zoom in on a detailed map of the few streets you are aiming for. The Renault system in the photograph is linked to a computer which also allows telephoning, monitoring of the car's performance and in-car entertainment.

Compact disks

Like video disks, the smaller compact disks (CD) can hold huge amounts of information. CD is now being used to hold databases. A single disk can hold several dictionaries and encyclopedias, and every entry is immediately accessible. This is enormously useful for such things as library catalogues or legal and scientific information.

△ The Domesday project divided Britain into 4.8km by 6.4km (3 by 4 mile) rectangles and enlisted schools and local groups to collect data about each area. Available soon on two video disks, any information about life in Britain today can be called up.

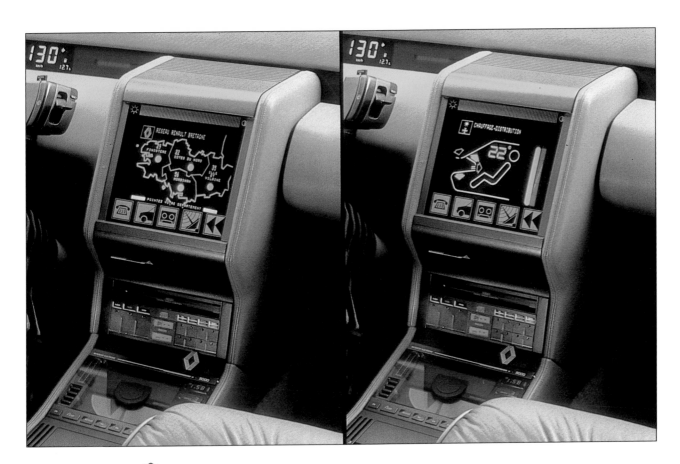

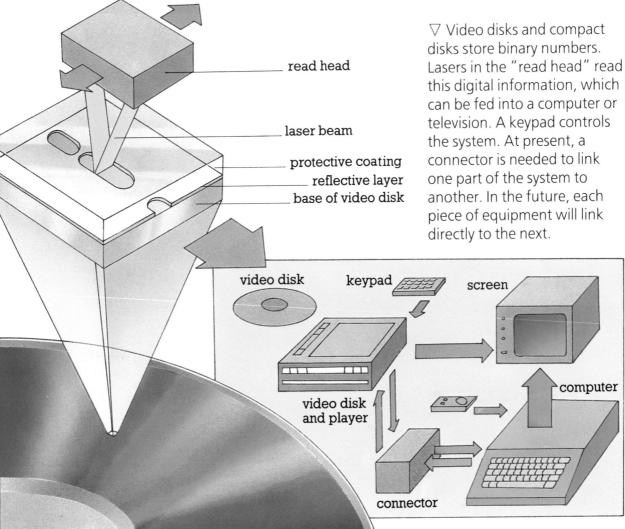

read head

laser beam

protective coating
reflective layer
base of video disk

▽ Video disks and compact
disks store binary numbers.
Lasers in the "read head" read
this digital information, which
can be fed into a computer or
television. A keypad controls
the system. At present, a
connector is needed to link
one part of the system to
another. In the future, each
piece of equipment will link
directly to the next.

video disk   keypad   screen

video disk
and player

connector

computer

Electronic publishing

Because IT processes images and text as digital code, new forms of publishing are possible. For example, in electronic publishing, "books" and "magazines" only exist electronically: readers receive them via computer terminals. They can read the material on-screen or print it out on their own printer. IT also makes "desktop publishing" possible. A single workstation has the capacity to process texts and images, design them into "pages" on-screen and then print them out.

Newspaper revolution

Newspaper and magazine production can be completely computerized. Reporters can write directly into computers, sending their text to the editor from anywhere in the world. Photographs can be sent by fax, or digitized at the head office. Because text and photographs are both in digital form, pages can be electronically designed on a page make-up terminal. The designer can rearrange, alter or change the size of text or pictures through the keyboard.

▷ Electronic publishing can also be carried out on a desktop computer. For example, the PageMaker program, run on an Apple Macintosh, will display the basic shape of the page. The designer can fit the text to the page, editing it where necessary. Images can then be placed anywhere on the page, in any size, to produce the most effective design. The finished pages are then printed out on the LaserWriter which is linked to the computer.

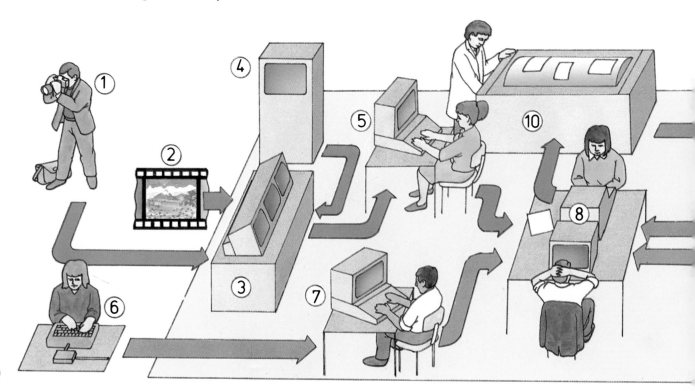

▽ A photographer (1) using video, or a picture agency (2), can send digitized photographs to the picture desk (3). A "frame-grabber" (4) freezes color pictures from television news broadcasts. A picture editor (5) selects images on screen and views pictures which have arrived as prints or transparencies. An out-of-office reporter (6) uses a portable computer to link up to the news desk (7). Sub-editors check copy on screen (8). The senior editor (9) makes decisions about the newspaper's contents. A scanner (10) reduces all pictures to digital code. A make-up terminal (11) designs whole pages on screen. Each page is stored by a central memory (12). Electronic signals are sent to an output terminal (13). A laser typesetter produces the local edition (14). The signals from (13) can also be sent to printing plants (15) throughout the country.

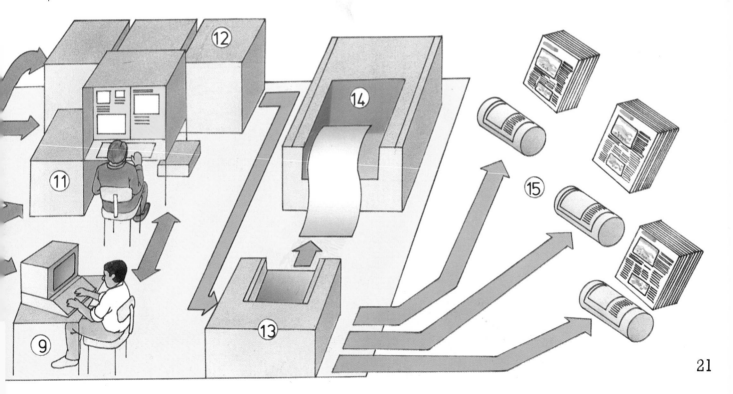

Computer graphics

IT systems not only process existing images, they can actually generate new ones. Existing images must first be digitized. Scanners like the "Scitex" can digitize photographs so that they can be manipulated. Colors and shapes can be changed and subjects which were not in the original can even be added. "Frame-grabbers" can capture and digitize individual images from video and television, and with "paint-box programs" the computer operator can alter or paint over moving video images. There are also "digitizing tablets" and other aids for drawing directly onto the computer screen.

▽ Computer graphics is very versatile. Images can be built up mathematically, or by using smaller shapes as building blocks, or by drawing. The pictures can be changed – in color, shape, light and so on – in very great detail.

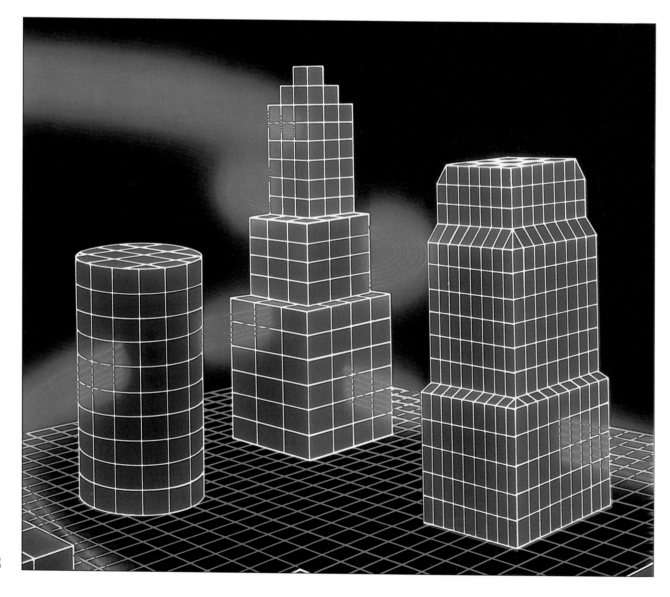

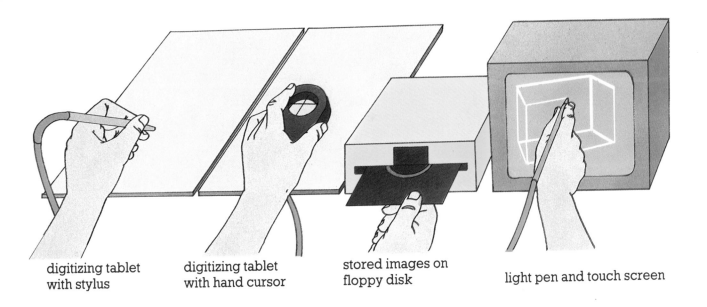

digitizing tablet
with stylus

digitizing tablet
with hand cursor

stored images on
floppy disk

light pen and touch screen

△ To enter images into a computer, designers can draw onto a "digitizing tablet" using a "stylus" or "hand cursor." The tablet contains thousands of numbered points which are digitally coded and make up the picture. All the picture information can be stored on disks, and the picture can be altered either by drawing over parts, or by entering instructions through the computer keypad. Light pens can also be used to draw directly onto the computer screen. The photograph shows a designer using a digitizing tablet with a stylus.

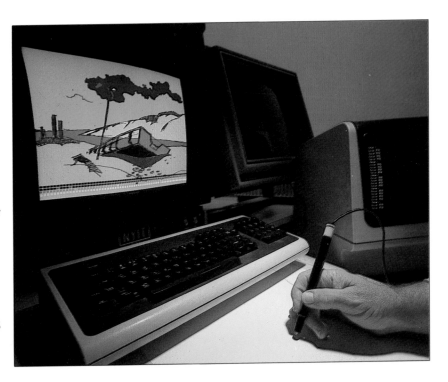

Computer drawing

Computers can create images in ways that are very important to IT. The most common is business graphics. Here, numerical information – such as sales figures – is translated by the computer into graphs and charts which are easier to understand. Computers can also generate animated graphics – moving images – like those in cartoons. Both computer games and film-makers use these. The computer can be given the beginning and end of a character's movement and will fill in the steps in-between. Color, lighting and position can be easily changed.

23

CAD/CAM

IT's ability to combine different types of information is very important in industry. Using computer-aided design (CAD), a whole product or a component can be designed on-screen before it is actually built. In addition, by using CAD, the designs can be tested by simulating real-life situations. Simulations can process vast amounts of data about the materials used and their properties. CAD can also compare or plan different methods of production.

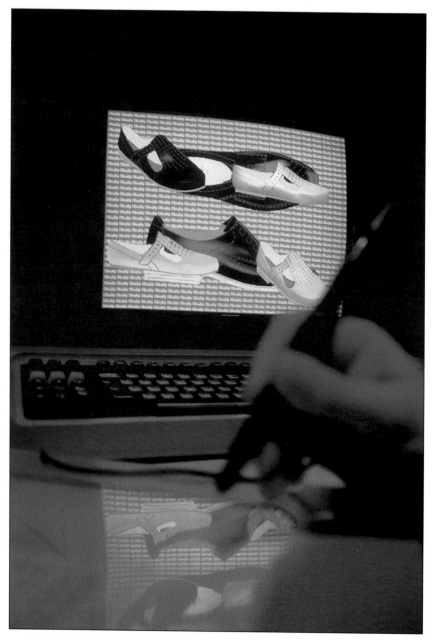

▽ Computers can build up images of complex objects by adding together simple shapes. These shapes can also be three-dimensional. This means the computer can hold a model of an object which it can rotate and see from any side. The computer can also add textures, shading and smooth edges. This allows objects to be designed and tested cheaply in the computer before expensive production decisions are taken. The photograph on the left shows how this technique can be used to design shoes on a computer screen.

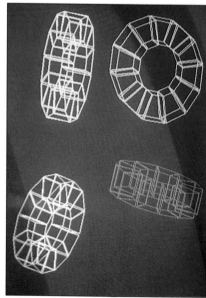

Computer-aided manufacture (CAM)

IT is used to monitor many different industrial processes. Information can be sent from any point in the process to central computers, from which instructions can also be sent. Digital systems are being used increasingly in industry to order materials and monitor production.

With CAD/CAM, industries are designing products and their production on computer. In the car industry, CAD/CAM is used to design and test cars and to send information to robots on the factory floor. Robots guided by electronic signals from a CAD/CAM system are capable of lifting, welding and spray painting.

▽ In the factory, IT can be used to instruct robots. This photograph shows spot welding being carried out by robots at a Ford car factory. Because the robots are controlled by CAD/CAM, their instructions can easily be changed. Potentially this means that robots can be programmed to produce cars to different specifications, changing colors, fittings and extras.

Expert systems

Computers do not actually think but computer systems which function "intelligently" are being developed. These systems are based on the knowledge of human experts and can tackle problems usually dealt with by scientists, engineers, lawyers or accountants. Doctors can already use an "expert system" to help diagnose illness. The computer asks patients questions about their medical history and present state of health. Using this information, it works out the most likely cause of the patient's illness. Another expert system called "Prospector" is used by scientists in the US to help detect deposits of minerals. Prospector collects data about the rocks and ores found in an area of land in order to forecast what type of valuable minerals might be found there.

Monitoring processes

Expert systems are particularly useful for monitoring processes. For example, they can collect data on metal fatigue, or the performance of an aircraft and decide when the aircraft should be called in for a service.

◁ Expert systems which are capable of playing chess were among the first computer programs to function intelligently. Programming computers to play chess is a great challenge: the computer must be able to choose from among a vast number of options. Tournaments are held between programs, some of which can beat chess masters.

An expert system which can be used on a small and portable computer is extremely useful. Tax or social security officials can immediately work out a claimant's entitlements by using a portable computer. The computer asks step-by-step questions to enable the officials to gather all the information they need to make a decision.

▽ The photograph shows how "computer vision" using tiny video cameras can monitor different parts of an aircraft. The computer can use this information to make expert decisions about the state of the aircraft.

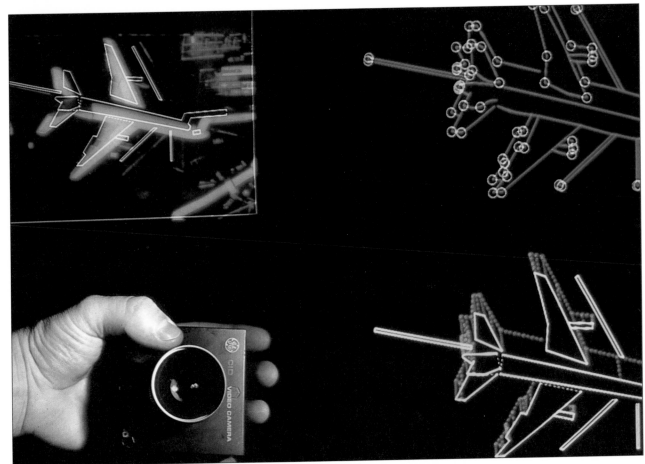

The future

The future of IT largely depends on two things: computers getting cheaper and more powerful and telecommunications switching to digital, large-capacity optical fiber. Both developments are already happening at great speed. As a result more homes and offices can now do their work electronically and can enter IT systems, both receiving and sending information.

Anything that makes a computer easier to use for non-experts is a gain for IT, and this is where much future development is focused. A great variety of computer programs which only require a little computer knowledge has already been developed.

▽ People will be able to talk to the computers of the future. The photograph (below left) shows an experimental computer being instructed by spoken commands. Compact flat screens will make computers far more portable. Telephones will be more like computers. The one pictured below can provide many different services such as a telephone directory and shopping facilities.

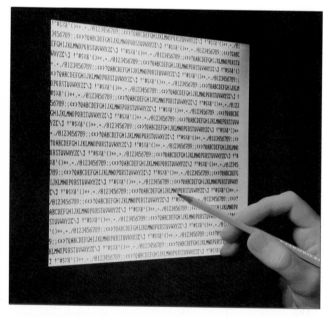

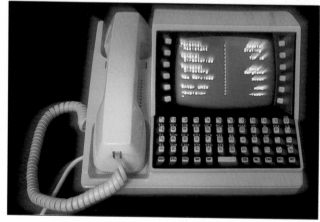

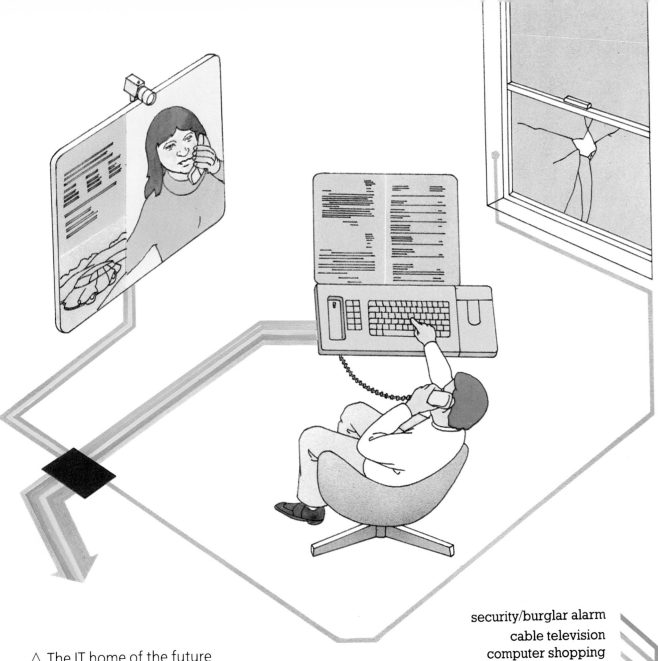

security/burglar alarm
cable television
computer shopping
video telephone
links to distant computers
electronic mail
banking

△ The IT home of the future will bring together many electronic facilities. Linked to the outside world by optical fiber, the system will handle home security and carry a wide selection of television channels. It will also allow shopping by computer and video telephone links using a flat screen. Connected to computers all over the world, people will be able to call up information, send electronic mail and do their banking from home. Although many of these facilities are already available, the IT of the future will link them into one compact system.

Computers of the future

The next generation of computers will allow users to communicate with the computer in normal language. Voice synthesis and response will allow the user to speak to the machine, dictating a letter or instruction, and be answered by voice. Computers will also become more compact as new "flat screen" technology develops. This also means that information on a screen will be easier to read and so working on a computer will be easier on the eye.

29

Datechart

1843

Samuel Morse sends the first telegraph message, from Washington to Baltimore. Fifteen years later the first transatlantic cables are laid.

1876

Alexander Graham Bell develops the first telephone in the United States.

1946

The first general-purpose computer, ENIAC, is built in the USA. This involves the idea of a single computer which can process many different kinds of information.

1948

The invention of the transistor at Bell Laboratories in the United States. The transistor is important because it introduces miniature electronic devices.

1962

The launch of Telstar in the United States, followed by INTELSAT I in 1965, starts the age of communications satellites.

1971

The age of microcomputing is made possible by the production of the first microprocessor using a silicon chip. Invented by Intel in the United States, it allows the power of computers to increase at awesome rates over the next 15 years.

1973

Britain launches the world's first teletext service, "Oracle." This sends information into the home alongside standard television broadcast signals.

1977

First functioning optical fiber cable is installed in Britain, followed one year later by the first public optical fiber link. The carrying capacity of this technology increases dramatically over the next few years, as does the rate at which it is installed.

1977

Video disk players are developed in Japan and the United States which use laser beams to decode information stored on the disk.

1979

Prestel, the world's first viewdata system, is launched in Britain. Though it gets off to a very slow start, it is followed by viewdata systems in many other countries, and is seen as the future of home information technology.

1983-86

This period sees an explosion in desktop computer power, in home computer sales, in the computerization of offices, and in the launching of new communications technologies.

Glossary

Cable television	Homes can receive television through cables rather than over the airwaves. Cable can carry many more channels and other information.
CAD/CAM	The use of IT to design and test objects, and to control their manufacture.
Convergence	The putting together of previously separate technologies: eg, telephone and computer technology.
Digital Information	Information which is represented in numerical – generally binary – form. Only digitized information can be processed by computers.
Expert systems	Programs that can collect information and make judgments and decisions.
Local Area Networks (LANs)	Computers, telephones, data storage, printers and other electronic equipment linked together within an office to form a single IT system.
Modem	An electronic device which translates digital computer code into signals which can be sent down normal telephone lines.
Telecommunications	Telephone-based technology for the electrical or electronic transmission of information. Includes telephone system, satellites, fiber optics.
Viewdata	Systems through which information can be sent from or received on adapted television sets, or computers, through the telephone line.
Workstations	Often described as desktop or personal computers (PCs), these are powerful microcomputers which fit on a desktop and can be linked to other computers and equipment.

Index

Acknowledgments

The publishers wish to thank the following organizations who have helped in the preparation of this book: Cumana Ltd, GEC Video Systems, IBM, Pitney Bowes, Renault, Standard Telecommunications Laboratories, Tandata Marketing and The Domesday Project.

Photographic Credits

Cover, contents page and page 13 (top): Telefocus; title page and pages 10 and 22: Tony Stone; pages 9 and 15 (center): Picturepoint; page 11: Rockwell International; page 13 (bottom): Pitney Bowes; pages 15 (top), 17 (both), 24 (both) and 28: Science Photo Library; pages 16 (left) and 28: Art Directors; page 16 (right): Cumana Ltd; page 18: The Domesday Project; page 19: Renault; page 21: Apple Ltd; pages 23, 26 and 27 (bottom): Colorific; page 25: Cincinnati Milacron Inc; page 27 (both) The Last Resort Picture Library; page 28: Standard Telecommunications Laboratories.